Pa Great Basket Caper

Paul's Escape from Damascus

Acts 9:1–25, 31 for Children

Written by Larry Burgdorf
Illustrated by Dave Hill

CONCORDIA PUBLISHING HOUSE · SAINT LOUIS

A couple thousand years ago,
A man named Saul went to and fro
He did the very best he could
To do what he considered good.

He was a man who had a plan,
And very quickly he began
To put all Jesus' friends in jail
And never let them out on bail.

But then on the Damascus road
He saw a brilliant light that glowed.
A voice said, "Saul, can you not see
That you are persecuting Me?"

The brilliant light was powerful,
The voice was so incredible,
The visions so immensely strong,
Saul realized that he'd been wrong.

Then all of life was changed for Saul.
He even became known as Paul.
His enmity came to an end,
And Jesus was his dearest Friend.

Now he told everyone, "It's true
That Jesus lived and died for you."
"He paid for all your sins," he said.
"And He is risen from the dead."

This so enraged Paul's former friends.
"Just think," they said, "what this portends!
If folks believe what they are told,
We'll soon be left out in the cold.

"If everybody follows Him,
Our chances will be very slim
To keep the leadership that's ours,
And we may lose all of our powers."

To solve this problem once for all,
The men decided to kill Paul.
They had some killers lie in wait
At each and ev'ry city gate.

Like many cities of the day,
Damascus kept its foes away
By building huge, high walls of stone.
One entered by the gates alone.

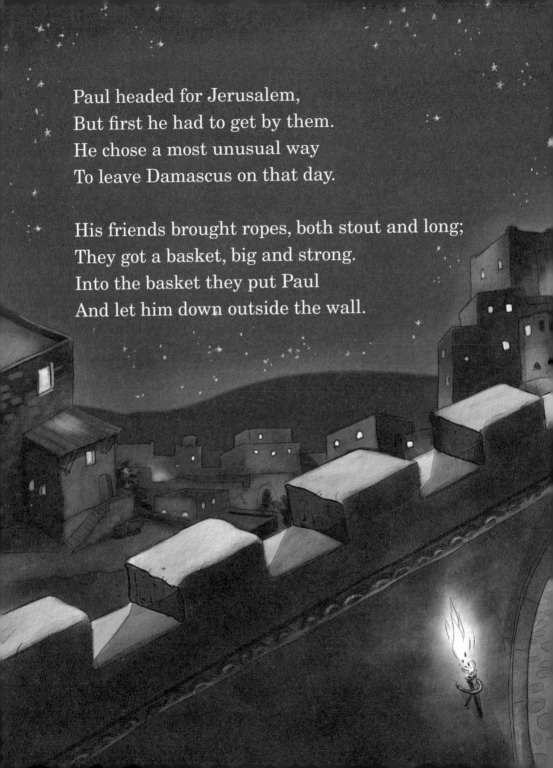

Paul headed for Jerusalem,
But first he had to get by them.
He chose a most unusual way
To leave Damascus on that day.

His friends brought ropes, both stout and long;
They got a basket, big and strong.
Into the basket they put Paul
And let him down outside the wall.

Think what a basketful that was!
It was so critical because
God mightily then used this man
To carry out His mission plan.

Paul sailed the seas and walked the earth
And preached for all that he was worth.
To earn his way, he'd sew a tent,
Then wrote half the New Testament.

Paul preached to Jews and Gentiles too.
He said, "The Savior came for you.
He died to pay for all your sin
And on the third day rose again."

That message still is sure and true,
For Jesus is your Savior too.
With faith in Him, you can be sure
That you're eternally secure.

Dear Parents,

A devout Jew, Saul believed he was only doing his job. Convinced that Christians were enemies of God, Saul made it his first and only priority to stop those who were spreading the Gospel however he could. The Jews and Christians of his day knew Saul as a passionate persecuter of Jesus' followers. Case in point: he was present at the stoning of Stephen.

It was a surprise, indeed, that this famous man had a sudden and complete change of heart. It took a visit from the resurrected Lord, Jesus Himself, to get Saul's attention. This man, who had been blind in his passion against Jesus, was now blinded by Jesus. And this transformation, in turn, got a lot of attention from everyone else. Until this moment, Saul's entire life had been one of misconception and misdirection. Now, his old enemies and new allies—the disciples— had trouble believing that he had become a believer. Paul spent several years proving the validity of his conversion and studying Jesus' teachings. Then he spent the rest of his life preaching, baptizing, training other disciples, and writing a great deal of the books we know as the New Testament.

His old allies were threatened by his new vocation, and because they shared the old Saul's convictions, they worked to stop his new ministry. This man who had caused great suffering, in turn, suffered greatly for his Lord. He was beaten, tortured, imprisoned, and persecuted. Ultimately, the only way to stop someone that passionate, well known, and outspoken is to silence him forever. Indeed, Paul eventually was killed for his work for the Gospel.

The lesson we can take from this story and from all of Paul's life is that God calls everyone to His kingdom, and anyone— even someone we think is unlikely or incorrigible—can be turned toward God. Nothing can stop the spread of the Gospel. To God be the glory!

The Editor